I0570322

CAW

POETRY BY A
MURDER OF WRITERS

Conceptualized and edited by Stasha Powell
Edited by Hyacinthe L. Raven

ISBN 979-8-9913131-0-0
ISBN 979-8-9913131-1-7
Library of Congress Control Number: 2024917471

Ix Studios
PO Box 45501
Westlake, OH 44145
https://ixstudios.net

All proceeds from "Caw" to benefit The Ohio Bird Sanctuary

Foreward

In the vast realm of the imagination, dreams intertwine with reality, where the mystical and the mundane dance in a delicate balance. Within this enigmatic realm, the seeds of creativity are sown, taking root in the fertile soil of the subconscious and blossoming into poems that captivate the soul.

Like so many great tales, this book's genesis emerged from the depths of a dream. In the stillness of the night, amidst the shadowy whispers of crows and ravens, an idea took flight, soaring through the corridors of my mind with a grace and elegance that mirrored the creatures that inspired it. Thus, a dream list was born—a collection of writers whose voices I admired and whose words resonated with me on a profound level.

What followed was nothing short of miraculous. Much to my astonishment and delight, each writer embraced the vision with open arms. This book is filled with those I love and admire making it all the more special. It was an honor to edit next to Hyacinthe Raven, a friend of many decades, who usually works alone. I appreciate her going out on a limb and helping bring my vision to life.

Here you will find poems interlaced with threads of darkness, mystery, and revelation. Each is a testament to the magic that lies dormant within us all. May these tales of blackbirds carry you to places beyond the realm of the ordinary, where dreams take flight, and the mysteries of the universe unfold before your eyes.

Welcome to the dream.

- Stasha

Chapter 1: Birth

S.A. Quinox

Creation

I looked for it
inside the palms of gods.
Hoping they would feed it to me
before I dared lick it from
their halls.

I ached for it to stream
downhill upon my shoulders
as if it were fickle like rain
before I dared drown myself
inside its wreckage.

But never had I thought
to find it staring back at me
from shattered windows
on sorrowful evening strolls.

Strength was sticking
to my skin all along.

Had I dared taste
its succulence.
Had I dared dip
my fingers
inside my ghost
before daring
anything else.

John Burroughs

Cause and Effect

A beginning can be
a beginning of winning
a beginning of tyranny
a knock-kneed travesty
a launchpad of love
and wonder and thunder
and it could lead one day
to sitting in your living
room at age fifty-seven
listening to Shitdisco
putting together a jigsaw
puzzle of a portrait of Frida
by Alfredo Arreguín and
wanting to cleanly break
with your commitment
to not drinking booze
for ninety days or forever
whichever comes first

A beginning can burst
like my mother's colon
at age sixty-five when
she was hospitalized
for pneumonia for the last
time and way back when
I spent nine months in
close proximity to that colon
becoming an eggy blackbird
in a membrane meant to break
and bound to lead
to evermore breaking

3

Christiane Knight

Perilous

It is perilous,
The passage from the safety of darkness
To a bright and unknown new world.
I have always been comforted by shadows.

They tell me that this is for the best:
I have been suffering, they say.
Life is supposed to be joyful.
The sun should shine on your path.

But I prefer the heart of the forest,
I dream of the rustling of wings.
I long for fog-shrouded evenings,
And the peace of silent dreaming.

I find this dazzling path confusing.
Let me crawl back to the undergrowth,
To the dusky spaces with crowded trees,
To the call of black birds from the branches.

Stasha Strange

Bleeding Bonds

If we'd shared the same nest,
she would have pushed me out
with no remorse.

Firstborn always overshadowed
by the next, who
ruled the roost.
The one who whispered
suicide in my ears,
and tried to take me out.
Hair cut off while I slept,
hot curling iron
between my thighs
Broken finger disguised
as an accident …

I have always known
I bring out the violence
in her.
I helped raise her,
I saved her.
All she offered back
was vitriol and hate.

There was never
a safe place for me
until I flew away.
No one ever told her NO
or stuck up for me
Or even suggested
she was in the wrong.

They said I was over-sensitive,
and in the next breath said
her mental illness meant
she did nothing wrong.

I'm mentally ill too,
Not that it's ever been accepted
as an excuse for me

I'm the oldest,
so I'm supposed to let things go.
Like the fact the last time I was home,
my high school sweetheart
was her lover and living with my folks.
No one warned me what I was about to walk into.

At the dinner table she said,
it wasn't her fault I was such a slut,
that she had no choice but to date my exes.

I moved away at 17,
chasing survival.

Her imagination is a far-fetched thing
I love her,
I do.
But she always makes it
her or me.
We know who *she* would choose,
which is why I have no home to return to,
no birthplace to visit

Firstborn,
least loved

Michael Cunliffe

5 Reflections On The Human Condition

1
Time stands still. Spermatozoon meets ovum
in the ageless reckoning between ticks
of the second hand.
Two joined as infinitesimal one within an instant
of time, now moving again: there is *Me*.

2
Foretime there was no me
yet tock of pregnant nanosecond
gave birth, from foetus then arise
in body abounding consciousness,
sentience, cognisance, will, a name: this is *Me*.

3
Swimmer #13,071,973 was fastest
but what if beaten to the prize?
Or a parent not in the mood that night?
Or a second cup of tea erroneous
flapping wings of a butterfly: what becomes of *Me*?

4
Should embryo formation deviate in any way
is this met hen a whole other me
living and breathing? This me another supplant
or awareness erased, utterly replaced,
and I'm gone? Not missed…never was: who is *Me*?

5
Unreasoned, this me sprang forth in human form,
not bird, not flower. Incidental,
other life sprang as fish or trees or mites,
and yet could I by chance have been me,
but a whole other being, living and breathing: what is *Me*?

Hyacinthe L. Raven

Now

It doesn't begin
with a word.

Silence is the space
and nothing else,
like the world isn't
sure it wants this
to happen.

But I am here.
I was already here.
And I want to say
that I will always
be here, but it
takes me a while
to figure out how
to get beyond
this moment and
BECOME, because
that's what this is,
right? A becoming?

I haven't needed
to test out these
wings yet, so the
sudden rustling
that parts clouds
and sends dust
and sparks flying
makes me hyper-
focused on what
I've just gotten
myself into: a

whole
cacophony
of
being.

Tara Vanflower

Áine – birth

I awaken, blackness all around me. It's cool and quiet. I inhale, taking the earth into my lungs. My eyes open and light explodes like dandelion seed, adrift on the updraft.

My fingers burrow into the verdant soil, black from ancient deaths that churned to new life. I whisper my love to them, long gone ancestors whose DNA has infused with my own. Electricity transfers from my skin, to their grave. I invoke the ghosts to sing. Sing with my breath, sing with my new flesh.

The black birds circle overhead, their cawing like music that carries secrets to dark places. To angels with the proclamation to save and serve.

The red mare, with nostrils flared, shrieks with my birth. I stand and go to her. Our hair is the same color. The color of menstrual blood. Rust. Fire-Dead leaves and marigolds.

My hands smooth over her warm muscled flesh. Her wild eyes look into mine. My sweet sister. My hands snake over her coarse fur. She stamps her hoof, her head jerking up as her mane lifts with the movement. I press my cheek to hers, whispering soothing words of comfort.

I climb onto her back, my fingers tangling in her thick tresses. The clouds part, the warm summer sun dancing over emerald fields.

We run. And with every footfall a flower bursts open. Spreading across the fields, calling forth bee and beetle, bird and hare. We ride until all the world is alive with color and perfume.

Kaytee Thrun

The Owls

Toss to turn, tumbling, as done
Had a dream last night
Perhaps a nightmare
Remembering owls and a friend who passed
For a moment, I thought it was you
Not letting tears flow
As they certainly should do
There was a sense of peace
That you might have caught from me
As my arms outstretch or are they yours?
The wingspan of the largest owl
Backdrops my view
Now, seeing it is not you
It is the death of who we used to be
The end of me being the one used or abused
The owl wraps me in her wings
Comforts my loss and releases my sins
Then flies away, letting me be born as she releases me into the world
Perhaps tonight dreams again, with fresh eyes, a fresh soul
And clinging tightly to a single forgotten owl feather…

Rachel M. Croce

The Fruit

Adam's rib snapped at birth—
the world swaddled blame 'round his twin sister
two plums came tumbling out
into a puddle of thick crimson envy
double the fruit of a mother's labor

surprised and warm, Momma tore
then faded quick into dark loss of memory
doctors flocked to prune our cords—

while I pushed to shove you
right
back
in

you, a pretty doll dressed for prize
and I, a son, the apple of their eye
I've spun words into hypnotic sedation
twisted ribs from which I came
preying on the offspring of Eve
I choked them into silence
void any sense of shame

Tara Shannon

Evermore

Your birth never was, and it lingers in my empty belly
Your life, forever the question that haunts my thoughts late at night
And your death…
I have no words
Only heartache
In a matter of hours you went from
Being
…and then,
You were gone

Born into thought
A made-up memory of, "what if"
That remains locked in my heart
Evermore

D.L. White

Wild places

I wish to wallow in wild places.
instead I'm slunk in pathless stasis.
Solitude, it creeps in dangerous;
loneliness seems so contagious.

I recall a time
too far ago to mention.
I'd rest my bones
on sea and sand:
sit, watch, and listen,

with zealous beats
a child's heart owns.

Full of hopeful premonition.
The world would speak to me
through twisting birds
and creaking trees,
bending their way to heaven.
It was all so special then:
easy, kind and innocent.
I used to wonder:
if I climbed the tallest tree,
would I be able to touch the moon—
if I reached Luna's light
maybe I'd reach you too?

Papa said: "She's in the stars. She's in the moon— there's no need to rise
farther. Just look up through the canopy and listen a little harder."

So, I searched for you
in leaky liquid places.
I lost little parts of me
in wild goose chases.

I gazed, with owlish eyes,
at every shooting starlight;
I wished upon each one
until my heart fell sightless.
I haven't seen your ghost yet,
or heard an angel sing.
And still I dream
of climbing trees;
moon rays upon my skin.

Grandma said: "Ignore papa, he knows not of such things. The moon, the stars, don't own her soul, her soul remains in you."

Emma Lee

An Ink-dipped Birth

A flicker in the corner of my eye,
its iridescence catches the sun,
moves from forest green
to black-filtered, eggplant-violet.
A flight feather, a strong shaft,
vanes flustered but intact.

I take it home, clean it, dry it,
carve the ending into a quill,
dip it into Oxford blue mixed
with midnight ink. Patient
as a crow dropping pebbles
into a narrow-necked pitcher
to raise the water level to drink,

I write. Steadily words build
the foundation for a poem,
pressure light to give letters
due thought. The page turns
blacker. Scatter sand to mop
up excess ink, wait to dry
before folding. An origami
bird with spread wings.

Ideas need to take flight.
Let your ink-dipped wings
absorb the script, flex
its metaphors, test the weight
of its heft. Let grief drop
like rain from waterproof
feathers. Birth is grief,
provoked as you leave
your creator's nest empty.

Lisa Taner

Weighed & Measured

On the outside it was interminable, watching this birth.
All hands on deck, with no doctor in sight, but patience filled the waiting area.
Time had lost its meaning. Moments, swollen to capacity, quieted the din.
This something new unfurled a curled beauty in its finite presentation.
Then, came the apology.
I'm sorry for taking your time.
As if we could not find the same patience he steeped himself in,
this brand-new patriarch.
On the inside, a world was held within the small, emerging figure
infused with all we could not know
with the exception that there was so very much to this being
years swaddled around him
and just now visible, wings below
ready to journey him on at a whim to his next plateau.
His son, now fully the caregiver, accepted the change
and pocketed it
quietly steering the old man through the exit doors
giving a nod of thanks to those of us marking time
We, witnesses to the birth
as the son manifested into something new and golden,
like a newborn before us, weighed and measured,
to see if he could answer life's calling.
We nodded in return with gentle smiles
welcoming him into the family of the unfamiliar.

Rachael Ikins

Oasis

Three red notes, cardinal, robin scolds,
and down the hill lavender dawn, crows mob
an owl, or an eagle from the balcony of 40-year-old maples

I use my camera like binoculars to try to see
what giant they are bombing into daylight, but
their voices build better architecture than the eye of my phone

A necklace of paw prints in snow describes
the perimeter of my porch like a line from a poem,
coyote.

When we stumped into the blue horizon, we smelled musk,
alpha male fox too-warm February morning, when the water
lay open a woman's mouth, but still the blue gills, the sunfish
sank deep into frozen mud, suspended animation, not coming
nor going

he crossed the road under a street lamp, he looked me in the eye,
black pupil, white light, his tail a question mark, his shoulders
promised a broken neck. I fumbled with leashes and gloves and
stumbled. He vanished before my camera opened its eyes.

Redwings swell ownership on thin, leafless stocks, where,other
days as we wander in that cloud of musk, we see a braided
trail-two stars. I wonder where they den.

I lie in bed at night, think of all the night creatures rumbling up
and down the cart-path, a teaming city of life, while we dream
with our guard down. That night I went to sleep, the front doors unlocked, the
porch as well. Anything could've dropped from
the universe

wheeling overhead on bat wings, three stars,
padding the stairs, pawing the windowsill,
carrying my heart in its mouth limp as a dead mouse,
still warm and clicking.

Chapter 2: Life

John Burroughs

Cause Célèbre

Consciousness is a road
rash mishmash
hoping to thrive
and dead or alive may not
exist in the sense that we think
except in sync with Pete Burns

Dead mom lives on
and live dad is dead
and what are attraction
transaction and every other
action but atomic reaction
and some birds fly and some
further than others and others
crash land either early or late
and some find no delight
in flight but intervals of time
are whispers in a whirlwind
and beginning and end
and you and all of them
are more than any of us
can begin to comprehend

Consciousness is a chemical
by-product wishing to be alive
or so this blackbird dares to surmise

And what if we have no
choice but behave as slaves
or, at the very least, agents
of oxidation, combustion
reduction and decomposition

Tara Shannon

Digging

I was digging
Long before I knew what I was digging for
I just always felt like there was something more
Beneath all the things that didn't seem right
All the hurt
And everything I didn't understand

There was so much I didn't understand

And I thought,

"Why is it like this?"

I dug harder
Deeper
Something was there
Hidden
Meant to be uncovered
…a version of me buried beneath layers and layers of unbroken cycles, fear,
fairytales, disillusionment
And lies

I chipped away at bedrock
Reshaping my very foundation
And it hurt!
Oh, how it hurt
But I kept hearing over and over in my head
How it would be worth it
So, I kept going

After a while, I wanted to give up
I was tired and my eyes were swollen and red from all my tears
A little blackbird landed on my shoulder

"Carry on, carry on, carry on"
It sang

So, I did
And so I do

Digging, hurting, healing
Living

S.A. Quinox

Consciousness

Your voice is like a lost lullaby.
You haunt my shadow.
You climb down my breath
and leave fingerprints on my skin.

I cannot name you.
Though, much like you,
I am just here.
Marching through the daze
of a life that isn't mine anymore.
Nameless and voiceless.

My world is skyless.
No bird spreads its wings here.
Rain rises from the bottom up
and soaks my soul gently.
Damp from my shoulders drips
like melancholy into palms, forsaken.

I am a mere apparition.
A castless shadow.
I cannot touch.
Yet I walk this earth
with restless feet and drowsy eyes.

Come.
There is madness in my breath
and I ache for embrace.

Stasha Strange

We share a melancholy heart

We share a melancholy heart
worlds apart.
We speak in sage
and second tongues.
Teeth and bone
with no judgments in sight.
I physically feel it when
the birds slip into night.
The pluck of a string
from their heart to mine.
Behind macabre sight
I see eternal struggle,
turmoil and torn tail feathers.
Dreams of unliving
but also, a magic not
yet allowed to fly.
One that would keep me
forever protected from
sing song suicide lies.
A life I tried to toss aside,
before the blackbirds
let me look through their eyes.
The starlings are flocking
against a bleeding moon,
as the ill winds whisper
to the stars I hear
the far-off dim call:
a murmuration
of my own salvation

Rachael Ikins

Last Night You Shut the Window when You Went to Bed

Moon laid his tongue on the earth
tasting ghost pepper. And your mother
patted a scarf around your face,
grandmother worried
about your bare legs,
you at twelve,
a creature of juice.

Fields, grass a sheet.
Glass fractured into code,
north wind's dagger.
Your mother wipes your nose.
You zip her into a puffy jacket,
fur-trimmed hood
up to her cheeks, her eyes turquoise
as new starling eggs.
A month before she died.

It's February.

A murder of three crows watches
your creeping trail
up the hill. You think,
I must bring them a gift,
Lego piece, a mouse carcass
in a Hotwheels car
stolen from your brother
twenty years ago.

Wind carves lines of poetry
into your brain
with Orion's blade.

Mother clutches a branch
her feathers blue/black,
your grandmother disappears
down the road,
small sparrow, homesickness
in her right hand
divining rod bobs a heartbeat
in her left.

Rachel M. Croce

Knocking

Through golden hourglass I watch a determined
flickering fumbling bumble bee
then attempt a self-soothing mumble
"be here now"
and note the tension swelling

I till nails into summer's bookend eve
the same fingers that dig into marriage
and baby's thighs
and natural family planning
until fragile limbs fling 'round my neck
as the smallest little bird starts pulling

I think how God must be a puppet master
lifting strings at each end of your laughter
as He paints my chin with silver
I watch you hunt crickets under stones in the driveway
crumbling dirt away from your body
between fading pink polish
seven inches from a Band-Aid

just for a moment
I almost forget
deep
deep
down
all I have is the memory
of that night I moved silently with you
the weaving of our fingers and the knocking of our knees
how it felt to be kissed on the ground of New England
between moss and balsam-covered sheets

Christiane Knight

Wings

It spreads inky-dark wings
With a raspy call that
Echoes off the trees.

A greeting of equals;
It knows its own kind.

I answer back with my
Best imitation –
Though I'm fluent in Corvid
My accent is bad.

The bird doesn't mind.

I came to the forest to
Clear my head
Dwell on my losses
Burrow into the mosses
Leave behind sorrow,
Begin again tomorrow.

The crow mocks me for this:
"Care no more for those who
Cause you pain! Give them not
A moment's thought.
Fly free, unburdened by
The weight of the world
Are we not kin?
Remember who you are."

A restless movement in
A dusty, forgotten corner of my heart
Stirs, roused by the impassioned scolding
From the feathered messenger.

Remember who you are.

I feel the shift.
The transformation begins –
Let me turn this darkness
Into wings of my own.

Lisa Taner

Life Flight

Combustible senses awakened by
the firecrackers of the unexpected
An emergency seat emerges
to extinguish and quiet crises
blinding your being
from glimpses of its true intent.

The nose of our plane
prepares to part the clouds
as that opportunity window
slides next to you
buckling you in.

You live in your head
wings clipped of true flight.
Here is a respite,
a full cup of soul
served from the beverage cart.

Your mask fails
to dull the temporal.
An aromatic orange
peeled adjacent
makes you prisoner turned disciple
in a tangible moment.

A sentence on the page before you,
the author's delicious bliss
of devouring the written word.
"I like...the feel of what has accumulated from before and what is beginning to
impend
Becoming surefooted on the highwire of the author's intention."
A sister
whose spirit moved you

to the emergency seat
before any words of welcome.
A high flying hour
transversing the knots
which have tripped you up
on the occasion your chosen path
dispensed all the altitude
to your shallow head
withholding oxygen
to the cells of your soul.

This is your May Day
this day you may choose
as with tomorrow
and those days which follow.

You move toward each horizon
and manifest the reality of this,
your personal flight.

Emma Lee

An Urgency of Words Written on the Sky

Moon opalled the dew
that shrouded the grass.
The dark hour before
dawn. Only the raven's eye
moved, rapid flickers.
Its legs seemed too spindly
for its weight. Cobwebs
sparkled like costume
jewelry for ghosts.
Shadows dimmed
the fake wonder.

Warmed, raven
spread her wings.
Her onyx feathers
shine like wet ink.
Aerial acrobatics
are not just to entertain.
Her song creates fog,
lines traced through
movements mimic
letters. The sun whitens
the clouds to a page.

Why this urgency
to write? A warning?
A story? A ferocity
of words. Rhythmed
by desire. A choreography
of form. A deathly
message. Who was it for?
Church bells
fluster the morning air.
Something or someone
is about to be erased.

Hyacinthe L. Raven

Instead

From up here,
it is immaculate.

The wind keeps me
blind to anything
that isn't myself,
but at this point
would I even
be able to
tell otherwise?

I am the sun,
I am the clouds,
I am the air
that fills both
of our lungs,

that keeps us soaring.

What if I
had said
yes when you
asked me to leave?
Wove patterns
into the sky as
a parting cry
and then watched
as you fell, wings
fluttering, an omen
to those left behind?

I know you wanted
that sacrifice, needed
it to be who you thought
you were, but no—

there is no glory in that,

not when every part
of you is part of me is
part of this beautiful
beautiful world we can
barely even hold for a lifetime.

Kaytee Thrun

The Ravens

My locks were long and deep midnight sky
They flowed out in waves and engulfed you in darkness
Thinking you were blissfully charmed
The day you walked into my life, my world
Your raven with dark dark hair
You brought me into your hidden lair
Tricking myself in control all along
My friend, my lover, my life, my months and years
Those days shall always sit in heaven in my memories
Yet nothing is quite safe or sane
It changes in an instant
So, like a dark bird, you swooped in and attacked
My hair knotted, my hands scratched and scraped
My world left bleeding
Wishing you had stayed
Wishing you would leave
Learning to love and stretching my black wings out to reach you, alas
You were too far gone away already
You left me alone, perched, broken
Now as a damaged bird of prey
We both were unable to fly, unable to keep loving
Only able to exist apart…

Michael Cunliffe

5 Reflections On The Human Experience

1
Time an enigma, days fly as milliseconds and years
rolled as one into cursory adventures,
myriad imaginings merged in a fleeting unity
and poured as juice into the sippy-cup
of a New World explorer: this is *You*.

2
Foretime no footprints appeared in this dust
until explorer burst forth into undiscovered lands,
a poetry of both destiny and recklessness
absorbed, photosynthesised and worn as capricious fashion,
a burgeoning self-identity: who are *You*?

3
Worker bee 13,773 down upon knees;
spouse, a sedan, 2.53 children, and an SUV,
mortgage weightier than third-world liability,
a no-longer-trim belly, ideals once free
now shackled to consumer identity: what became of *You*?

4
Divergent mouths kiss no more,
accord split as superannuation in two,
horizons of yesterday's dusk reimagined as joyous solitary dawns,
expensive bottles of wine once saved for special occasions
now zealously gulped, leftovers poured down a drain: where are *You*?

5
With earnest 'goodnight', pot-plants at twilight
Are lonely old friends shut away in the greenhouse,
muttered memories half-forgotten
upon comfy-slipper trudge down the cobbled path,
back to an empty bed scarcely enduring tomorrow's sunrise: is this *You*?

Tara Vanflower

Macha – life

This is war! Fight, fuck, bleed. We burn until the light dies. We churn the soil over and over and over until every nutrient is consumed. They will extinguish the fire. The furnace of your heart must ignite! Keep burning. Keep burning. Keep burning. Keep burning. You will die.

Watch my crows feast. Hear them caw their battle cry. *Fight. Fight. Fight. Fight,* they scream. Keep burning. Keep fighting.

See the sky turn black. See the sky turn blue. See the rivers run red. Burn. They're coming for you, those birds with their shiny black feathers and black beaks. They're coming to feast upon your spent flesh.

Fight and burn. Keep burning. Your body is a furnace, burning the fuel of your heart. Keep feeding the fire, black coal into the pulpy red furnace. Feed the fire. Take the light while it's yours. Fight the turning of the sun. Don't stop. Burn. Until the last flicker, the last spark of flame, goes out. Fight and fight and fight. Clutch at the sky. Take everything that's yours. Bleed with men. Fight with men. Grow and twist towards the sun. Let the vines of your fingers grasp out and take. Let your mouth taste the blood in every living thing. Let your voice sing to dead stars. Let your flesh meld to flesh, heart to heart, tongue to tongue. Scrape at the earth, burrow deep, take the soil in your hands and grow flowers. Break bones and bodies. Birth heavens and hells. Paint dreams with your blood and love. Fight against the spinning. Fight against dying. You are a furnace of finite fire. Feed the fire until there is no fuel. Become green and verdant, air, and light, and sea. Call forth beings into existence. Live in their light. Fight. Fight. Fight. Fight. Fight.

D.L. White

Mi Vida

My body is his altar;
he pays homage to my curvature.
Carves a songbird from my chest:
Hallelujah! Hallelujah!
Lay me to rest.
Mi Vida, my life,
lay me to rest.

No mercy can be given;
daddy's belt begins to sting.
No sin can be forgiven—
The song bird mournfully sings:
Hallelujah! Hallelujah!
Lay me to rest.
Mi Vida, my life,
lay me to rest.

"I'm a bad man, bad man,"
he laments as his love breaches
my borders.
"I'm a bad man, bad man,"
he bleats as he beats new colour
to my cheeks.
I drown in his self-loathing.
Chase death for release—
and the white dove
flaps its wings…

Te extrano
Te iubesc
I accept him as my other self.
Hallelujah! Hallelujah!
Lay me to rest.
Mi Vida, my life,
lay me to rest.

Hallelujah! Hallelujah!
Lay me to rest.
Mi Vida, my life,
lay this love to rest.

Chapter 3: Death

D.L. White

golden

I see you golden
in gardens of grey,
hope spilling from your chest,
praying for redemption
for sins you didn't commit.

What lies beneath your breastbone?
Does your ribcage bloom
with curious life,
or is it a dead nest?
Corpus delicti.

Do the remains of love haunt you?
Does it stick to you like gloss—
or does it bleed
from old wounds;
plaster you with your past?
Do you feel massacred
or nurtured
by it?
By me?

Will you hold me until it's over?
When a sickle-man knocks three times.
When my bones creak
towards oblivion,
will you let love hold them together
while all else is breakage,
is wreckage,
is rubble—
will you worship my ruins?

Just before my mortal passes to afterlife:
can we lay down and stare at stars?
Will you name them after my scars?
Will you spin with me
under a canopy of trees,
and watch autumn strip little wings
from cooling branches?
Will you let the lucky leaves bury me—
in golds;
in reds;
in oranges;
in October blood.

I wish I could be golden like you:
unafraid of endings,
of creeping darkness.
Does the darkness confide her secrets to you—
or is it light that gifts you such divinity?

Can we visit all the places you're scared of?
So I can be the hero for once,
and you the dithered damsel.
I heard once, that you know your grave
when you see it—
that it's covered in shadows and voices
and blinding light that only you can see.

You were my love,
my life,
my light,
and I think you'll be my grave.

Lisa Taner

Beloved

What is it our beloved gives?
A lightness to lift our laughter
A strong hand when we need comfort
A familiar face
with years of our history
behind each glance

What is it our beloved gives?
A cradling of knowledge
of our particulars
Favorite colors
The side of the bed we claim
Seeing our best
Our worst

In this way
we walk through time together
until that time transitions

And then, what is it our beloved gives? Its weight has shifted
but it is unchanged
All that we've seen before
now witnessed through eyes that are wider
A sight that has expanded
to see within our hearts
to lessen the weight in our minds
A grace descends
to find its place at our very base
lifting memories made together
where we may stay forever, side by side
So we can still whisper to one another
in the quiet of the night
in the reflective light of day

What is it our beloved gives?
It cannot be contained
It cannot be made plain
It surrounds us as before
though we reach out sometimes restive
at a loss with thoughts
that it is not where it always was
And yet
It is.
For our beloved was once a single star
- and now, a galaxy.

Michael Cunliffe

5 Reflections On The Human Impermanence

1
Time, silent watcher, impartial and directionless
as scurrying cockroaches, the light switch flicked,
spotlight upon stage – final bow –
gasping crowd – mouths open yet no words escape
then time's thumb downturns: *Now* becomes you.

2
Foretime this trampled, worn dust once dynamic
until ticking hands wore thin, wore brittle
and pieces began to snap, pieces began to fall
and dust sat heavy on a clock's shoulders as decay
unbrushed, unnoticed – cacophony of neglect: *Now* waits for you.

3
Psalms 13 & 7 & 73 chanted, gatekeepers to a crypt
long forgotten, slipped from a theistic mind adrift,
amid adoring crowd, bowed, in faith worshipped,
text preached, idolised, yet of life stripped
faithful and unfaithful alike, devotion merely postscript: *Now* commands you.

4
Five toes, slipper'd and cracked and peeling
in disinfected hospital bed, five shuffling
toward eclipse of cognisance – mere blink,
without reopening – passing from one's own reckoning
into pregnant unknown: *Now* watches you.

5
Christ, Allah, Shiva, Odin, Hecate, Zeus
arm-in-arm, watermarks, observers as finite droplet
slides down uncharted yet well-worn drain;
curtain drop but a footbridge to soil enriching worm-food
six-foot underground: *Now* is gone.

Tara Vanflower

The Morrígan – death

Come to me.
Close your eyes.
Lay down your battle.
We open our arms to you. We hold you in our arms.
I will kiss your dry lips.
I will smooth my hands over your broken body.
You are sweet in your dreams.
A perfect white rose, perfumed, silken, with emerald thorns.
Lay down your vessel.
Sleep.
The black earth awaits.
The birds gather to pick your carcass. Your bones stained red from battle. One
day you will be diamonds.
My precious daughter.
Kiss our lips. Your breath is mine.
When you sleep you will know everything.
When you sleep, your battle is won.
One.
Your battle is One.
Awake from the dream. Hear the banshees sing for you.
My birds carry your soul with them in their coal black eyes.
You are the oily shine of their feathers.
Your voice is their voice.
The sky is your home now.
The lightning streaking through the rain.
The rage of the ocean.
The single drop that carves the mountains.
And when the light returns you will bloom no more.
Dream and dream and dream, until the spark ignites again.

Rachael Ikins

Personal Ad: Must

Like long walks on the beach
to bury the bodies. Must have
a sense for subtle fragrance,
denouement. Skilled digger, far enough
from the water, ocean claws back all
of our leftovers

for the crabs.

Leave hair clips, buttons and can-tabs for crows.
They thread sprigs of rosemary through tab rings
with beak and claw, drop them like May Day baskets
on doorsteps of those they like.

Don't piss off crows. They remember forever, dive bomb
as sweat drips from your nose into the crypt you excavate.
They scream "Fuck! fuck! fucking murderer!" jealous perhaps,
you usurped their word,
murder.

Wear a necklace—blades, shovels, trowels,
Japanese pruning saw
the kind that folds in on serrated teeth,
an Army knife, corkscrew for long walks on the beach.
Be prepared.

Elderly couple across the street from the path to
the ocean collects Girl Scouts and paper boys, secret cookie
addicts, innocent as Mr. and Mrs. Santa Claus,

until someone's dog breaks out of a fence, digs up their back
garden, lured by the siren of baked goods left too long,
those obscene giant rose bushes.

Wear big coats with lots of pockets, hide shoes, hats,
false teeth, paper airplanes from busybodies.

Seeking cat lover. Or cat.
To bury the evidence or
fling it in reach of tide's fingers,
cats studied slaughter since first wandering
into that Egyptian granary several thousand years ago.
They bring us bodies,
broken in their mouths
for love.

Kaytee Thrun

The Vultures

Picking at my dying carcass, you were
For nearly a year after you had left me
You made empty promises that you would return
But each night, the bed stayed ice cold
Like my exposed tendons and bones
In my foolishness and my youth, blindly believing your words
How the young mind whispers such sweet words in your head
Spinning out the badness
You just continued to pick away at my ridged skeleton
As you needed me and the death in me allowed it
With love and fear, and fear of love in me
Confused by what remains you see
Bit by bit until there was nothing
No bit of flesh or speck of me left
Then one day, you were just gone,
Fooling myself with logic, but it was foolish words
You left the broken remnants of my soul behind
No stitches in the world could put all of it back together
It would take pinching on stitch at a time
Year after year leaving thick red forever scars
Binding the pretense of pretend skin over the me still dead
As they healed slowly over time, the rest of the vultures circled
Only my soul still alive, they wait for me…

Hyacinthe L. Raven

Then

The moment it
happens, I am
completely unprepared.

Maybe I'm shot.

Maybe I'm caught
in a crosscurrent.

Maybe I'm suddenly
heart-stoppingly
just done here.

I expected something
like static on the
tv, a crackling in

the background that
would eventually
fade to the way
black sounds.

Or maybe

I expected something
like the Cocteau Twins,
a softly drowning
chorus of angels
blanketing me til
I forgot I still
needed to breathe.

But no, this is
a din, it is
the sum of me,

and even now
I
am
too
much.

Emma Lee

Return to Dust

The crows are raucous again.
Thinking against their noise
is exhausting. I remember.

I don't know the name
of the dead one, but they mob
it, peck it as if it might resurrect.

I was mothered from a pool
of blue, blue ink, sculpted
into my shape. I remember.

Each crow has a dead amygdala.
It's a logical reaction, one crow
calling another, another, a crowd.

Did I have a father? He was ghost.
A blank page, a series of folds,
these aging wings. I remember.

The crows check for danger,
for further death. Perhaps they
fear becoming the next victim.

I edit and edit. A futile search
for the perfect word. Flight feathers
on a skeleton. I remember.

The crows bounce, undisciplined.
Scribble a mess of lines, tangled
like scattered, wind-bruised petals.

Vanes preened to follow the lines
of thermals. An eye, a cauldron
of morning. I remember.

A silence grows after the fluster
of exiting crows. A lotus can bloom
in muddy water. The moon, calm

as a stone. Air settles. I watch.
Death, like birth, needs silence.
An unread poem. I remember.

Paper wears thin through frequent
reading. I'm tired. The best we
can hope is someone remembers.

Christiane Knight

Death: A Song

Once I was beautiful.
Now they wrap a faded cloak around me,
A pathetic comparison to the
Proudly tattered blackbird's finery
That I once wore:
Long skirts my sweeping tail,
Wide lacy sleeves fluttering like wings.

I always preferred to sing.
All of these words have been
Put forth before in song.
You've surely heard them.
But now I can only croak;
My voice is weak and hoarse,
A faint gasp when compared
To the robust song of my youth.
Still, one day in the future
You will remember my song.

The tune has changed as well.
Formerly impassioned and plaintive, now it
Grates in one's ears, remarkable only
For its insistence:

I am here
Do not forget me
Once, I lived
Do not forget me

Carve those words upon your heart
One day, they will be yours

S.A. Quinox

Cessation

Another day runs past
my frozen apparition.
My breath aches, clogged
inside my throat, and
I dare no longer grasp
the gravity of my feet
roaming this world, lost.

I've ached and I've bled,
but no soil ever bloomed here.

I've dug and I've wept
but no flower ever reached
the surface.

My coffin lies still
inside the dirt of your embrace.

The sky no longer holds me,
and my name has withered from your lips.

This body has finally come
to connect with something, after all these years.

And I, will forever ache
to find solace, or a glimpse, if at all.

John Burroughs

Cause of Death

An ending can be a mending
a rending and emending
an upending of all intending
and a chore you might perform
while listening to Gang of Four
on your office floor drinking
decaf and craving a cannabis gummy

It can make you a mummy
give you relief or make you gloomy
find you eating cheese puffs
focused on headlines and deadlines
fixated on pain and *Seinfeld*'s Elaine
wondering how many years remain

An ending can sing to you
like your mother's Bee Gees
records on a console stereo
before any of us could know that
even compact discs eventually degrade

An invasion of death
is an invasion of life
which always results
in something dying

And crying and sighing and flying
are a circle of suchness and is-ness
that is endless as nobody's business

And a blackbird can't fade
to black when it's already that

And we can't die if we are never alive

Rachel M. Croce

Broken Wings

Wilting like a single stem out of water
baby sister meticulously fawns
a beardless chin tucks into cigarette-stained wings
with cocaine nails, he plucks at wires across black wooded hollow
crow's feet stamp the corner of each eye
while brass strings drag at the tip
from the ground up, his voice rings
singing Blackbird song

pause
press
pluck

pause
pull
peck

tones drip from his lip
into a bucket
like the one Sal carries
I carried them toward Hosford Pond
on a sled past the shed through vines
the rope he pulled wrapped tight
the same strength that pinned me down in the basement
spitting chewed-up words into my mouth
as bundled fists forbid to me sing
until Momma's voice loosed his grip
and set me free
as free as one could be
with broken wings

Tara Shannon

Without You

I walk with you in shadows late at night
In that liminal space that bends and blurs between dreaming and waking

We can speak here. You and I. Sometimes without ever needing words. Only thoughts.
Feelings that cannot be described through any combination of the 26 letters contained in our alphabet

We reminisce
We chat about what you've missed
We imagine what could be
Dancing on moonbeams
And fairy lights
Sitting quietly in the dark
Sipping the tea we spill

One sugar and one milk for you
Nothing for me…
I'm sweet enough

You laugh

Oh, how I miss that laugh
I try my best to scoop it up
Filling my pockets
So it might last the hours spent
Living without you

But then, the constant *caw* of the raven outside my window bleeds into your laughter lifting me away from the shadows and into the sun

My pockets empty

Stasha Strange

Word came on raven's wing

Word came on raven's wing
that your smile had dimmed
forever.
Grief washed over me.
Us of the dark eyes, stormy skies,
and things not meant to be.
Teenagers torturing words together
lost in sleepless days.
Our hearts not on the same page.
You wrote me beautiful,
beyond any truth I knew.
I threw your words back at you
through that crowded kitchen,
heart in my throat,
slipped my way through.
There were no words
that could make me love you
the way you loved me,
But in tortured flight we flapped on
singing the same cruel song,
Blood on beaks
with wings clipped. You flew off with a murder,
I chose an unkindness
I'm always better in a pair
You always shined in a group
Your smile lit up night skies
Now in melancholy disguise,
shroud of regret
at our last conversation.
We wrote again,
together,
you and I,

just months ago
As easy now as it was difficult then
my crow feathered friend.
What ifs are now no more.
I wish I'd heard your laughter
one more time.
Now just silence that
aims to strangle.

Meet The Murder

Christiane Knight is an artist, musician, writer, and author of the contemporary fantasy series *Stories of the Eleriannan*. They have been published in a variety of small press 'zines.

https://www.christianeknight.com
Instagram: @christianeknight23

D.L WHITE is an Anglo-Irish novelist, writer, and poet. He has published several works, from poetry collections to full-length novels.

Outside of writing, he finds joy with friends, family, books, and thoughts of travel. He is a committed advocate and ambassador for mental health, working on a volunteer basis to support people with their battles, having battled his own demons his whole life.

On the subjects of birth, life and death, he has been quoted as saying, "I did not choose any of these things but I shall make the best of them."

Instagram: dlwhite_author
Threads: dlwhite_author
Facebook: D.L. White
TikTok: dannyboywrites
Twitter: DL_White_Author

Emma Lee's publications include "The Significance of a Dress" (Arachne, 2020) and "Ghosts in the Desert" (IDP, 2015). She co-edited "Over Land, Over Sea," (Five Leaves, 2015)

https://emmalee1.wordpress.com
Facebook: https://www.facebook.com/EmmaLee1
Twitter/X @Emma_Lee1
IG: @emmainleicester
Blue Sky: @emmalee1.bsky.social
Mastodon: @Emma_Lee

Hyacinthe L. Raven is a poet who splits her time between Cleveland, OH and Davis, CA. Her work has appeared in publications such as Not Dead But Dreaming, Thistle, and Blackbird. She has been the editor of Via Dolorosa Press since 1994.

John Burroughs served as the 2022-2023 U.S. Beat Poet Laureate and is the author of The Wrest of the Worthwhile and Rattle & Numb. He is the founding editor of Crisis Chronicles Press.

https://linktr.ee/johnburroughs
Instagram: @crisischronicles
Threads: @crisischronicles
https://www.facebook.com/JesusCrisisBurroughs
email: jc@crisischronicles.com

History of Kaytee Thrun. My love affair with creating began as a child spending every afternoon in my parent's floral and antique shop. As the only daughter of artistic parents, my eyes were always able to see the beauty and potential in even the strangest things. On one trip to an auction with my parents, we came home with a rickshaw, a wicker coffin, a king's sword and scepter, and a laboratory skeleton. Many days like that one fueled my sense of imagination and eccentricity. Having released multiple books and albums, the journey to combine words and images to master a "novel-in-poems" never ceases. Drawing from my past doing fine art fairs, the desire to collaborate with other visual artists, photographers, and crafters is a form of hypnosis, and it has me under its spell. At this juncture of my life, finding my own extraordinary side has been a journey. It is with great hope that you find a piece of my work that will inspire you to be who you are. "Remember to thank those who inspire you."   - Kaytee Thrun, Glass Half Full Goth®

https://linktr.ee/kayteethrun

Lisa Taner is a native daughter of California. Her love of written language was nurtured by her mother and maternal grandparents. With an education in journalism, her early writings morphed into stories, but poetry has always remained the origin of comfort and connection, a touchstone for her relationships with people and her place in the world. Lisa lives in the San Francisco Bay Area with her husband and son, and hopes to compile an American perspective/memoir of her experiences visiting Turkey over a 30 year period.

Michael Cunliffe sprouted from an alien seed pod rumoured to have been scattered in the Scottish Highlands by the sons of the notorious Ragnar Lothbrok around a thousand years ago. At an unknown point in time he found himself transported by some little-known form of alien technology to the strange lands of Far North Queensland, Australia. Later in life he became a hippie, grew his hair long, drank schooners of ice-cold beer and listened to articulate neo-Grunge Rock artists. Now he enjoys peace and quiet. And he writes poetry. Quite a lot of it, actually.

Rachael Ikins is a queer 2016/18 Pushcart, 2013/18 CNY Book Award nominee, 2018 Independent Book Award winner, & 2019 Vinnie Ream & Faulkner poetry finalist. 2021 Best of the Net nominee, 2023 2nd place winner Northwind Writing Competition. A Syracuse University graduate. Author/illustrator of nine books in multiple genres. Her writing and artwork have appeared in journals world wide from India, UK, Japan, Canada and US. 2024 will release her new young reader book The Magic Blankie (Clare Songbirds Publishing House). Cyberwit released her poetry 2024 collection A Handbook for Alchemists.

Rachel M. Croce considers herself a creative with her preferred medium being people. Born into a family of fourteen, she developed a love for the art of relationships, yet holds formal training in the science of them. As a Couple and Family Therapist, she currently owns and practices out of her northeast Ohio business, Stone Mill Couple and Family Therapy. Rachel enjoys integrating anthropology, psychology, and philosophy with wilderness and art therapies. Standing in as a witness to others' emotional healing, she began creative writing as a way to process her own emotional turmoil. She uses her blog as a space in which she is able to break down and distill her own inner process. Rachel's writing has been published in the Ohio Bards Poetry Anthology and Psyche Magazine.

https://thewordmill.blog/
https://www.instagram.com/the.word.mill/

S.A. Quinox is a young Belgian poet, philosopher and a student of the paranormal. She writes for the broken among us. Quinox is a beginning yet growing poetess that is known for her beautifully deep yet melancholic words which have the ability to wreck your heart and then glue it back together again. At a young age, she had already discovered her love for writing. What first started off as suicide notes later on transformed into the poetry she writes today. Quinox has a unique way of designing her own books. She always chooses black pages to preview her style. By doing so, she makes her readers delve deeper into the abyss of her words.

Besides poetry, she also aspires to be a spiritual person. Quinox enjoys learning about the paranormal arts and takes classes from professional masters. In daily life she finds a lot of pleasure in connecting with nature and animals.

Quinox loves to respond to messages so please do not shy away from conversation!

https://facebook.com/SAQuinoxPoetry
https://instagram.com/QuinoxPoetry

Stasha Powell, known by her pen name Stasha Strange, is a distinguished writer whose creativity is fueled by the untamed worlds found within books. Her spellbinding prose graces the pages of prestigious publications like Poetic Reveries Magazine, Ohio Bards, an Anthology, New Beats Generation, Blossom, an Anthology, Setu Journal and Sidewalk Sanctuary her debut chapbook. Stasha's adventurous spirit is shared with her partner, Andrew, and her beloved animal companions.

https://linktr.ee/stashastrange

Tara Shannon is the creator of Rabbit & Bear. She writes about her journey with cancer, trauma, anxiety, depression, grief, and hope.

Facebook and Instagram: @tarashannonwrites

Tara Vanflower, known for her hauntingly beautiful vocals, has been the voice of the darkwave band Lycia since 1994. Beyond Lycia, she's a creative force, expressing herself through solo albums and venturing into literature with novels like the "Violent Violet" series.

https://taravanflower.bandcamp.com/
https://lycia.bandcamp.com/
https://www.amazon.com/author/taravanflower
Instagram: @tara_vanflower_lycia

www.ingramcontent.com/pod-product-compliance
Lightning Source LLC
Chambersburg PA
CBHW060348130626
46553CB00003B/1131